i exist

by sydnie short

3

"as above, so below
as within, so without."

-    *the law of correspondence*

sydnie short

table of contents

¹the hermit

---

[1] the hermit is a major arcana card in most traditional tarot decks that point to a time in our journey where we look inward and withdrawal from events to gain higher insight and clarity.

i'm a writer
so, my bad days aren't just bad days
they're red lights that refuse to turn green
a december in love with summer suns
and no matter how much time passes
they never reach each other

i exist

inevitably broken
an undying cause
a lions roar
gnawed up and outspoken

i feast on thunder and tremble on its lungs
yet, i'm louder
i am angrier

you and me

we exist
as strangers
moments in-between brokenness
as saviors
gods
mothers
victims

all a crisis that distracts us from ourselves
that we feel so alone and empty

when this is all over
we'll owe the biggest apologies to ourselves
for staying so deep in our mistruths

when the streets cry out *hallelujah*
with suns i can't bare
a reality i can't tare
i rest upon the silence in the morning
life's cavities swallows me in pieces

life never fully breaks you all at once

it's always little by little
day by day

summer souls in a winter body
california in paris
the dichotomy
the split that deadens us

inside us is one thing
yet, we portray another
the burden of identity
and trying to release the boundaries

somedays existing feels like i'm scorching
under the sun
wrestling with the unavoidable
the unchangeable
all the things that i can't control

an unending desire for things
that feel so out of reach

money
      real love
            real intimacy

but on days like this
when i'm feeling like a sore thumb
a warm bath becomes my savior
a hot cup of tea becomes my sanctuary
and as unpredictable everything may seem
some of these may just be moments
that get perceived as eternity

somedays existing is soft
lullabies on my tongue
and if you step back
you allow things to be things neither good nor bad
just moments
in the dual planes of life

until the bath grabs you by its teeth
and swallows you

i caught a glimpse of the sky
as it birthed tomorrow
it's 5 am
and my tongues dry

mind in a high
you never want to get down from
i can feel time collapsing
dissembling
in my palms

as it weeps i faintly hear it whisper

no matter what it will always be today
we're always in an infinite now

maybe if i had an ocean for hair
trees for skin
grass for eyes
birds for thoughts
maybe i'd feel beautiful
maybe i would stop praying for my world to end

maybe the questions would impede

do you ever get outraged at existence?
other than the fact that we're here
why did hate have to exist?
pain and suffering?
why?

i question existence more than my faults
are we really lost?
or were we all misguided
just to be left a stray
to be so far from ourselves?

spoon fed a controlled truth
blind to our power
prisoners to fear

how to destroy a child:

construct an image of who they are not
and who they were never meant to be
then as they try to morph into the mold
you break them
you realize they'll never be who you want them to
be

shame em shame em shame em

unsubscribe your subscriptions of love
gaslight them
shred them to the point
to where they cannot return to wholeness

shred the desire for change
of doing anything that resembles
personal freedom
so, they remain directionless
swimming in a love drought
and broken in the palm of fear

she exists as poetry
a swollen thumb
in a fist
a marshmallow tongue
a room full of angry people

she exists
as an ache
in a back
overworked
tired
        weary

she exists and she doesn't want to
she
is me
and i
feel like giving up

what would the moon say about me?

'you roam around in chaos
unaware of the flower you're blossoming into'

no one else can see life the way you can
their world could be upside down
and you would never know
there are somethings you can't see

their wars look like sunsets to you
your freedom, their hell

scorpion sun
hang lining in my room
the endless cycle of life and death
simultaneously combusting in my lungs

the daily demands of life i reinstall into my memory
sip my morning cup of aches and pains
recipe created by the devil themselves

sometimes a generational curse
are the beliefs passed down
that we never truly believed in

i drink my sorrows
brush my teeth with rum
this daily metamorphosis makes me numb
when does it end?

a long piercing cry leaps out my chest
momma said *hush baby, inside voices*
ever since i kept my voice soft
held it inside all my life

sometimes i feel like i must ask permission to be me
or to feel something
to be validated
to love and to receive love

eyes
heavy with sights unseen
thoughts bleeding
thoughts in the emergency room
in critical care
too fragile for a dangerous mind

does anyone have a clue on how to make it better?
reality has been stepping on cracks
breaking my back

wish i knew where i was headed
do i finally free myself in the end?
from whatever this is…

21

it feels like tug of war
something is pulling me in
while something is pulling me out
they are both strong
both heedless winds
but who is stronger?

i feel the dying need to be nothing
neither happy nor sad
the empty
the numb
a face on a milk carton

or the love and light
maybe i can get another chance in another reality
maybe i'll be a little stronger
have more reasons to keep going

note to self

deep inside your heart
you hear it
a peaceful voice itching for change
can you hear it?
what is it asking of you?

my 9 to 5 makes me dizzy
makes me want to split my head open
there's just no soul in my day
everyday i go home and want to claw my eyes out
because i wake up to a cycle
and do the same thing repeatedly
to what end?
but maybe it's not just the 9 to 5
it's the choices

wrong or right
the ones i didn't make
or the ones i did
everything that led me here

the shell of expectations
cracking under pressure
the weight of who i am or
who i have been or who i'm supposed to be
and when i want it all to stop

when i beg the world for quiet
when i beg the world for peace
i go mad at its silence

as it whispers
the only way out, is in
the rage in my tummy growls
how it tells me it's famished, that it's lonesome
and bathing in so much anguish
rage is pain
rage is the face front of powerlessness
and even though my 9 to 5 makes me dizzy
makes me want to split my head open

it's really my war cry for peace
my hunger for power
and the mere confusion and distress that violently
stands in between it all that splits me open

24

no headlights in the morning
our goodbyes will have to wait
our goodbyes refuse to fall asleep
our lies know everything

where the hell am i going?
who am i becoming?
my thoughts seep out
thirsting for remedies to my
ceaseless innermost void

i exist

somedays broken
somedays somewhat together
i lost the instructions
how do i be me?

what's next? is this right?
god it's me, can you save this number?
i'll call again
i just need a friend
some direction
hope
anything please?

i'm drained participating in the day-to-day life
on autopilot
get up, raise your hand, get credit on
being a decent human being

i'm drifting soundlessly
a far cry away from home in the ocean
life is this huge mystery
yet here i am drowning
being guided by a faint light inside
telling me i'll be alright

[2]**death**

---

[2] a major arcana card in most traditional tarot decks that can mean an ending, transition, or rebirth.

i have many names
yet, i am no one
a poet
a daughter
a sun
i am faithful to external identification
and dishonest to my truth

if i can crash into every lie
and set it ablaze with my lonely
i would always find myself burning

my whole life i bit my tongue
posed
maintained composer

i'm learning anger is a secondary emotion
rooted in fear
sadness,
and powerlessness

so, instead of making myself smaller
i'm exploring it

in what areas of my life do i feel powerless
internally?
how do i find it externally?
what am i truly afraid of?
how do i react to it?
how do i hide it?
what are ways i can feel in control?

-   *shadow work*

what role do i play in this world?
every part of me feels fictional
i know nothing and it petrifies me
but it also enlivens me

our whole existence is imprisoned
imprisoned
by our perception

what if we can expand?
what if we can think new things,
bigger things?
what would existence resemble?

the hierophant
the beliefs
the walls
society didn't have room for too many prisons
so, they decided to create it in ourselves
doomed at birth
with false truths
marauding down our throats

i believe in something different
yet, i put a warning label
like i'm ashamed to think for myself

it comes with a price
freedom comes with a price
you must own it
if you're going to be free
in a world of mental prisons
you need to stand firm

the tower will shake you
the white horse will take you if you do not
but the world will thank you

the destruction is strategic
meant to catapult my metamorphosis
and sometimes i'm too calcified to break
but breaking can be riveting

when you fall apart
you see what isn't working
darkness is light that needs love
don't shame it
transmute it

can't escape the noise
even when you dim it

your silence will scare you love

existence doesn't have to be stagnant
when i close my eyes
i am a phoenix
with fierce rosy raging wings
rupturing into the sky
i paint worlds inside of cold wars
making it rain marmalades of colors

when i get away from the noise
from the world
sit my ass by a tree

i pretend
delude myself in a daydream
and then it stops

i no longer must feel the things i don't want to feel
i am no longer the person i don't want to be
i am no thing
i can be a phoenix
i can be anything
when i remove my attachment to anything
that isn't me

to live you must die
echoes inside my inner wind
my inner world
and i did not always understand that phrase
yet, i did not always understand
how easy it is to trap a soul

our whole lives we're fed some catastrophic
narrative
of the end
of death

eternal shame, guilt, and fear
so deep, we feed it to our children
we manifest it in our daily lives
so anxious of an unknown we can't see

now the collective subconscious fears leave us
ignorant
afraid to metamorphosize
afraid to know how to surrender

death is not the end
it's an end
a transition from one to the next

the death of self is a releasing
a surrendering of all that you hold
that was never yours
all that keeps you from your wholeness
from your divinity

rainbow bodies
bones paper thin

when i drive i am an eagle
with bullion wings
like a stampede of bulls
steady
444
666
what does it mean?

free falling into heaven
into a bleeding blue
as the wind gnaws on my eye

so, you're an old soul?
show me your past lives
show me your scars

how far are you from yourself
that you keep searching
keep on living
in this decaying timeline?

are you chasing god?
a thought
a moment in time?

is it for peace?
is it for love?
who are you mourning?

what blue do you bleed?
why do you keep on fighting in this war?

i always labeled myself as an observer
i would sit
watch the world and eat my popcorn on mars
confess my dreams to the moon and the stars

there are something's your parents can't teach you
because they are still learning themselves
how can someone teach you about authenticity
when they're living a dream that's not their own?

my forte all my life has been authenticity
how can i be me?
in a world surrounded by people who aren't
themselves?
and of course, i didn't have the answer

so, sometimes i bite my tongue
put myself in a box
and that discomfort i sensed all my life,
that followed me everywhere i went
was me out growing some boxes
outgrew the label of 'weird'

i am indescribable
a tall tower with stars marching into black holes

i must get comfortable with being uncomfortable
i won't let projections and illusions be pushed on me
i am immense
and brilliant

i am the container of infinity

note to self

when the universe knocks you off your feet
it's not cruel or mean
our perception labels it as mean

sometimes it's getting you to a place
where you can finally allow
what it needs to do
so, you can be at the place you're meant to be at

if you control it, you'll play it small
or play it safe
and no matter how safe you play it
how worried you are

you are frightened of staying where you are
don't let illusions start feeling like home
what's next is not known

create your future from your truth

sometimes i wish i was pretty
like how the moon and stars say i am
or do i wish i just felt pretty?
or do i wish i lived in a world
that didn't make me feel like i wasn't?

why do we care so much about the wrong things?

we imitate god
as if our hands could compare
like our black and gold-stained fingertips
are enough
we slap ourselves and create new eyes

we drown ourselves in comparison
to meet expectations
we created ourselves

and if we ever tried to lift our naked lips
and whisper to the sky
let there be light
light knows not our voice
our voice could never shake heaven

strawberry girl
drenched in oil
relinquish your anger onto me

a knight at my window proclaimed
he had chunks of midnight on his armor
his blade deep into his chest
pain is an illusion in a lover's mind

our whole life we remain strangers
from trees
to the earth
to ourselves
we are a part of the whole
yet, blind to it

we were told hell was an after story to blind us
to the reality that we're unconsciously creating it

when it all falls apart
new can grow
new can begin

the death me of happened within
when it all fell apart
a root sprung out of my womb
the seeds planted in my sides
eager

jaggeder teeth in a hungry wolf's mouth
it's time
to destroy the split that was created
on a false foundation
on a false god
that allows the lack of accountability,
fear, and pain
to mask our consciousness

³*judgement*

---

³ judgement is a major arcana card from most traditional tarot
decks which is asking you to realize and embrace a higher
level of consciousness, as it serves your highest self.

have you destroyed the radio that
resides in your head
that's broadcasting nothingness?
your delusions and dissatisfaction
with yourself and the world
have become your meals

i'm a poet
we will never see the world the same
i create worlds

you see trees
i see pillars
that reach their hands into a wounded sky
with stars brighter than you and i

you see houses with families that have smiles
sunny like july's
i see castles with bricks stacked like crowded teeth
filled with beasts

fallible
ravenous
and no matter how profane they think they are,
they all look the same
lost

i'm a poet
i create my world
yet *the world* creates clones
creates vacant beings
living a fiery death
they relive over and over again

your success does not inspire me, your joy does

you only fall backwards into the vacuous abyss
you created because your chaos comforts you
it's not your fault you were born into a false premise
a nightmare
with eyes wide
it's not your fault
but don't you fucking dare accept nothing
that doesn't sit right in your core

march
lay your head on a pillar of stars
the stairway to heaven closed
you didn't come here to play stupid
don't you dare forget your power

46

life's agony has shown you all things you are
and things you are not
look inside yourself with separation and awareness
of that which you are not

you are not what you are experiencing
and are not the things you've been told
you are merely an awareness
an infinite stream of consciousness
experiencing life

47

the anger you hold
is borrowed
you can give it back
the fear,
guilt,
and shame
you can give it back
it is not yours
that weight on your shoulders that you feel
that relishes in your spirit
it is not yours

you are everything you need to be
release yourself from your conscience

you are free
and you no longer need to give yourself
permission to be happy
you no longer need to give yourself
permission to do the things that make you feel alive

you no longer need to want to die
just because you truly want to live
there are things in this life
that require nothing from you
the more you focus on the things
that truly lift you up
the more you will bring them to you
the more your days will fill with joy,
light and spirits of abundance

-    law of attraction

49

note to self

you're too attached to who you have been
change can't happen
who you want to be cannot become

why are you not enough for yourself
that you search for everything
that you have inside of you, in the world?
in half empty lovers?
and if you know why,
when will you be enough?

what you want from others that you're not giving to
yourself, will create more illusions
of temporary satisfaction
until the voice inside
that you've dimmed and crippled
gets so loud that you get uncomfortable everywhere
you can't sit still
it's the gum in your belly

love isn't pain
there are growing pains of it
when you're faced with a mirror
everything you are trying to silence
or are unconscious of lays right before you
for judgement

love is the awareness that peers light through
any part that needs more of it
yet, the more you break yourself
you'll create more opportunities to see why that is

break the illusions of self
then the illusions in your world will to

you believe
if you dim yourself
the inner noise won't be as loud

nothing scares you as much as being small

but you're not scared
you're petrified
if for a second you no longer give attention
to how you saw yourself
and give as much energy to how far you've come
and who you are becoming
you would only see that you are great
and nothing else
and right now, it's not a matter of if you are great
it's a matter of when you will allow yourself to be

bend
   bend
      bend

until you break

      move
    move
  move

until you shake

you
a puppet
the world
the ventriloquist
how you let exteriors determine how you feel

one click you're angry
one click you're sad
how you feel is valid, but you have control
protect your peace
you owe yourself that

you're betraying yourself
when you turn down your brightness
you're a sun paying a light bill
you're being lied to
you're forgetting your power

whether we are aware of it or not
we are a part of something bigger than us
and we've been taught to be small
live in hatred
fear
and control

what happens when we love?
who can judge?
who is bound to vanity?

the point of everything
is for the expansion of ourselves
the unlearning
unwinding
and reteaching yourself that you are bigger
than what you have created yourself to be

who you desire to be
is an extension of who you are at your core
change can be terrifying
but not living in the fullness of your potential
is scarier

we come here to create and to learn
let the dissatisfaction and circumstance
be the fuel to where you want to go

you control the narrative
the story can be whatever you want

so, create, breathe
become alive in the way you came here to be

55

"*you are asleep, unconscious of the god within and the god without. the goal is to wake up, to become conscious of where god is within your life and connect to it.*"

-   unknown

"*the person one grows into is a mask warn over consciousness. in the awakened, the consciousness shine's through*"

\-   unknown

don't lose sight of who you are
because you're surrounded by people
who aren't who they say they are

falsities in another narrator's life
if you're healing
finding peace
you're doing what people
spend their whole lives trying to find,
themselves
please be proud

58

she has golden eyes
sapphire lungs
a ruby
a jewel
the skull of a thousand ancestors
she is time
an explosion of energy
how beautiful she is yet she still aches
a mystery and a reformatory
a magnificence in agony
blind to the treasure inside

in the dark
when you slumber, you heal
you transmute

fall into your darkness
fear is holding you back
you will overcome
you will transcend time
create a limitless pit within yourself
the source of your own light

if you just fall
let go
of time
yourself
your attachments are what's holding you back
in this darkness
open your eyes
you will stay dark until you can see in the dark

- *meditation*

when you choose the world over love
you start to live in a world looking for love

note to self

the realness in everything
is in as much as you can perceive

62

silence only scares you
because it forces you to meet the stillness
that stirs inside
the hurricanes, the hatred, the anguish

listening to what you've been overlooking
you haven't been okay, and that's okay too

but what's not okay is living in your mistruth
being small
you cripple yourself and dim your brightness
because of fear
what are you afraid of?
how can we stretch our horizons beyond it?

you're a mirage of something remarkable
your inner being is
a beacon of light
nothing can shed your armor

this world will try to shred you
it will test you to see if you are
who you say you are
or give you a chance to see who you are not

are you ready?
your comfort cripples you
yet, your discomfort crucifies you

pain was never meant to be the destination
just a tool to get you there

- *spiritual journey*

you no longer need to break yourself
to fit inside the mouth of the narrative
that resembles who your trauma created
you can change
you can free yourself
you can let go

let's take a deep breath
and feel the growing pains from all the times
you had to be a parent to yourself
i'm sorry beloved
you've been the parent and catastrophic child
for so long that you're confused
and waiting permission to feel

breathe

give yourself permission to heal from wounds
that you put too much pride in to break from
you owe yourself peace, love, and joy
you owe yourself to receive the love from yourself
that you desperately want from others

note to self

you must release yourself from
characters and narratives
from worn-out storybooks
that were meant to teach you
don't attach yourself to any pain
from anything that meant to be a lesson

you're trying to be something again
you don't even know how to *be*
how to sit still

you bite your tongue on stillness
sit your ass down and watch the clouds
watch how they don't have to be nothing
but themselves

you gawk at the girls on the moon
scowl at the red blazing petal
that dances in the midnight rain
you weep under suns that refuse to dry
you cling to everything outside of you

you are too far from yourself
too outward you are
free yourself within
you are magnificent
have you told yourself that?
have you seen your strength?
the strength that creates suns?
have you seen how bright you are?

what's inside is where you praise
a box full of mysteries
the world can't see you
if you can't even see yourself

you so desperately wish to save others from
the same nuclear war
you have yet to overcome yourself
playing god with lovers that feel like strangers
stop falling short of yourself

show up for yourself the way you do for others

we all ask
why are we here?
and i believe we spend more time questioning
than actually being here
vacant bodies
absent minds

our souls linger around as an accessory
nothing exists in you
life is happening for you

not to you
life is an energy
a mystery
a genie in a bottle that doesn't grant wishes
but creates the playground
for you to live out your desires

you've found yourself
yet, you still feel lost
that's because where you are
is not where you should be

birthed out of a dying womb
incapable of adoring you
as you lay under fragmented hues
healing yourself
you shine
bright
and beautiful

how dare you let others tell you
you are not good enough
that you are not worthy
that you are anything less than amazing?

how dare you forfeit your power
call it back

the crack of a tree branch
the cry of thunder
the break in the wind
you are a gazelle
fearful at that
wincing at everything
living in survival

become aware of everything outside of you
not just the chaos
the beauty
the skin of trees
the sky before it falls

the role you play
ask more questions
step outside of the you
you have created
and breathe

[4]the world

---

[4] a major arcana card from most traditional tarot decks which may symbolize ending a cycle, a change, and a sense of completeness.

i
have a beautiful soul
she's kind and warm
a cup of warm tea waiting for you at the table
angel wings with no body
she holds the essence of purity
and remains frameless

a smile with no bones
you just love being around her
you want to see how she'll take life in her hands
and create new stars
new love
new meaning

she's a breath of fresh air
she's my first love
she's one of those hugs that makes you want to
pack your bags and just live in them

and i'm so happy to finally
take the keys out the ignition
take my foot off the gas
and finally, be home
she's my home

- *homecoming*

be aware of the roles you play
the names you hold
the treatment you allow
to feel safe

be conscious of the love you accept because it
resembles the suffering you are used to
remember you will try to chase
what you're familiar with
even if it hurts you

learn to release the things you say to yourself
that you were told in your upbringing
you can choose to accept it
you can choose to release it
release what is not yours

75

like water in the wind
you can't bring tomorrow with you
no matter how hard you try
you must learn how to step out of the crust
of that which isn't you
the agony
the anxiety
see it as a friend

your separation to yourself and others will create the
largest pain in you

connect
even if its uncomfortable
to parts you shame
avoid
or run from
allow them to be the bridge
to an awareness of you that embodies authenticity
and love

note to self

your new life will cost of your old one
you can't be the person you were meant to be
by being who you have been

note to self

when you're stuck
confused about your purpose
ask your this
if you weren't afraid, what would you do?

note to self

*"if you ask for peace and prepare for war
you get what you prepared for"*

-     *unknown*

thank you for connecting with me on my journey. these poems were written on days when everything felt like they were falling apart, and these words felt like the glue keeping me together. i've pondered existence for as long as i've been aware of. i've struggled with mental health and purpose my whole life. now i'm on this beautiful journey of love, growth, and awareness that allows me to reshape the mold that i grew up in, into a formless beauty. i broke away from what i knew, to follow the inner light guiding me to wholeness. it was not easy, to step into the unknown but sure is rewarding. thank you, a million times, for being you and being here right now. i love you so much.

simple things to add into your day

- focus on your breath throughout the day.
  focus on the inhale, then pause, and then one
  exhale
- look at the areas of the most discomfort in
  your life and look at what they are asking of
  you
- be aware of your thoughts and the beliefs
  you repeat and ask do they reflect your
  highest good
- try to embody the essence of that which you
  want to bring into your life
- eat nutritious meals
- allow time in your life for fun
- surround yourself with those who have goals
  that align with your highest good
- allow yourself grace and forgive yourself
  from the past
- do something different each day
- be aware of where you feel emotions in your
  body. give it a shape, color and then imagine
  releasing it into the earth
- ground your body
- cleanse your space

- try eft tapping in the morning
- trace your meridians
- move your body in ways that feel good
- free write or daily journals
- write from your future self and give your present self-motivation
- speak lovingly to yourself, see yourself through the eyes of a loving friend
- be honest with yourself and ask. yourself where in your life you aren't authentic
- show up as your true self and speak your truth
- learn color therapy and or sound therapy
- look inward for solutions, gratification, and meaning, rather than externally

sydnie short